Kay Gardiner and Ann Shayne

- 2. Introduction
- 6. **RIB LACE SCARF**
- 10. Lace Charts 101
- 12. **TUMBLING BLOCK LACE SCARF**
- 18. **CLERESTORY SHAWL**
- 26. **APERTURE STOLE**
- 34. Lace du Jour
- 36. **MOOD CARDIGAN**
- 46. Meet Jeanette Sloan
- 48. Abbreviations

INTRODUCTION

THE ENGLISH LANGUAGE uses the word "open" a lot. It has many meanings, some purely metaphoric. We speak of open minds, open hearts, and open hands. We thank a friend for being open with us, and a host for opening their home. We "leave the door open" when we are pondering new possibilities, or we can't quite make up our minds.

While we often knit with the intention of making a cozy, embracing fabric to keep out the cold, there is one kind of knitting that aims for openness, for letting light and air flow freely: lace. We create openness in our knitting by making intentional holes, which in turn form patterns.

Jeanette Sloan, the designer for this Field Guide, hails from England, where knitted lace has a long history. Jeanette likes to focus on contemporary interpretations though. Give her an old lace stitch guide, and her creative flood gates open.

On the pages that follow we present five of her designs: two narrow scarves that help us get our yarnover and chart-reading skills up to snuff, a triangular shawl that is worked sideways (and features the two lace patterns you can practice first by making the scarves), a stole that melds traditional lace patterns into an abstract surface, and a cocoon-like cardigan that can be worn two different ways.

Whether you are a longtime connoisseur of lace or new to it, we invite you to join us to imagine—or, shall we say, open yourself up to—the possibilities!

Kay   Ann

RIB LACE SCARF

Design by
Jeanette Sloan

START HERE. This skinny little scarf is a portable workshop in knitting lace. It features the Big Four of lace knitting: knit, purl, decrease, yarnover.

The rows are short so that you can quickly tink back and try again if by chance something doesn't look right.

Note that this scarf can be worked in a fingering weight yarn and also in a gutsy aran weight. Sometimes you're feeling delicate, sometimes feisty. Choose the yarn that fits your mood.

Once you get the hang of the Rib Lace pattern here and the Tumbling Blocks Lace featured in the scarf on page 12, you're ready to tackle the Clerestory Shawl on page 18, which combines the two.

KNITTED MEASUREMENTS

6¼ (6¾)" wide × 72" long
[16 (17) × 183 cm]

MATERIALS

Light Fingering Version:
— Helix by La Bien Aimée [100 g hanks, each approx 710 yds (650 m), 75% Falkland merino wool, 25% Gotland wool]: 1 hank Lise (A)
— Size US 8 (5 mm) needles, or size needed to obtain gauge
— Blocking pins

Aran Version:
— Merino Aran by La Bien Aimée [100 g hanks, each approx 182 yds (166 m), 100% superwash merino wool]: 2 hanks, Aimée's Sweater (B)
— Size US 9 (5.5 mm) needles, or size needed to obtain gauge
— Blocking pins

GAUGE

Light Fingering Version: 18½ sts and 27 rows = 4" (10 cm) over Rib Lace, using smaller needles and A
Aran Version: 17½ sts and 24 rows = 4" (10 cm) over Rib Lace, using larger needles and B

NOTES

Instructions are given for Light Fingering Version first, with Aran Version in parentheses; when only one number is given, it applies to both versions.

For Light Fingering Version, stitches are cast on and bound off using 2 strands of yarn held together in order to add extra weight to each end of scarf; the rest of the scarf is worked using 1 strand.

You may work the Rib Lace from either the text or the chart.

STITCH PATTERN
Rib Lace (panel of 29 sts)
- *Row 1 (RS):* P2, [k2, yo, ssk, k1, ssk, yo, p1, yo, k2tog] twice, k1, k2tog, yo, k2, p2.
- *Row 2:* P8, k3, p7, k3, p8.
- Rep Rows 1 and 2 for Rib Lace.

SCARF
- Using smaller (larger) needles, long-tail CO, and 2 (1) strand(s) of A (B), CO 29 sts. Cut second strand for Light Fingering Version.
- *Set-Up Row 1 (RS):* P2, k7, p1, k9, p1, k7, p2.
- *Set-Up Row 2:* P8, k3, p7, k3, p8.
- Continuing with 1 strand of A (B) only, beg Rib Lace; work even until piece measures approx 72" (183 cm) or to desired length, ending with a WS row.
- *Next Row (RS):* P2, k7, p1, k9, p1, k7, p2.
- Join second strand of (A) for Light Fingering Version.
- Using 2 (1) strand(s) of A (B), BO all sts knitwise.

FINISHING
Weave in ends. Pin to measurements and steam block. Allow to dry completely before unpinning.

Rib Lace

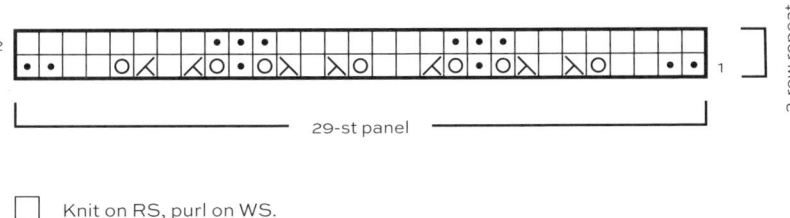

- ☐ Knit on RS, purl on WS.
- • Purl on RS, knit on WS.
- O Yo
- ⧄ K2tog
- ⧅ Ssk

LACE CHARTS 101

We admit it: At first glance, a lace chart can look like a tangle of symbols. But it takes only a little while to decipher what's going on, and once you do, it's a game changer—easier and more intuitive than working lace from written instructions.

For example, here are the written instructions for the Rib Lace pattern used in the Rib Lace Scarf on page 6.

Rib Lace (panel of 29 sts)
— *Row 1 (RS):* P2, [k2, yo, ssk, k1, ssk, yo, p1, yo, k2tog] twice, k1, k2tog, yo, k2, p2.
— *Row 2:* P8, k3, p7, k3, p8.
— Rep Rows 1 and 2 for Rib Lace.

Below is the chart for Rib Lace, which provides the same information in a more compact form and also shows the relationship among the stitches in a way that words can't. The key to the symbols is at right.

Each square is a stitch; each row of squares is a row that you work. For Rib Lace, all we have are knit and purl stitches, plus one type of increase and two types of decreases.

At right are some extra tips to help you understand—and work from—lace charts in this Field Guide.

☐	Knit on RS, purl on WS.
•	Purl on RS, knit on WS.
O	Yo
╱	K2tog
╲	Ssk

Rib Lace

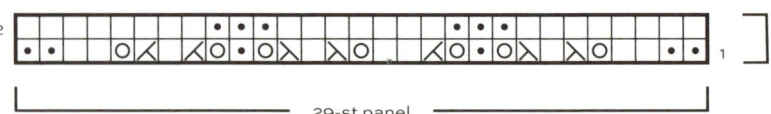

TIPS FOR READING THE LACE CHARTS

— Take a few minutes to get to know your chart and key, and compare them to a photo of the knitted project.

— Numbers on the right edge of the chart are for RS rows; numbers on the left are for WS rows.

— Work all RS rows from right edge to left, and all WS rows from left to right.

— The position of the number 1 tells you where to begin the chart.

— The chart shows the stitches as they will appear on the RS. Be sure to refer to the key to see how the stitches should be worked on both RS and WS rows, because the same symbol will be worked differently depending on which side of the work you're on. For example, in the charts used here, a blank square means knit on RS, purl on WS. And a black dot means purl on RS, knit on WS.

— Start slow. What feels unfamiliar at first will quickly become easier with practice.

— Color-code your symbols to help you catch the distinctions—for example, blue for a k2tog, red for an ssk, etc.

— Use stitch markers for marking repeats.

— Use a sticky note above the row to mark the row you're working on. That way you can compare the row you have just completed with the row you're working on to make sure that your stitch pattern lines up.

TUMBLING BLOCK LACE SCARF

Design by
Jeanette Sloan

How often do you get to make a five-foot-long scarf with only 26 rows? Here we see what happens when we cast on 278 stitches, then settle into an angular tumbling blocks lace pattern.

The amazing thing? When you've finished one repeat of the stitch pattern—26 rows of yarnovers and decreases—you're done. Whereas the even-numbered rows of the Rib Lace Scarf on page 6 are all worked as knits or purls (admittedly, a nice reprieve), this scarf requires working the lace stitches on both sides. The result is a scarf that looks cool no matter which side is showing.

The pattern includes all the information you need for using two different weights of yarn.

KNITTED MEASUREMENTS

65½ (66¼)" wide × 4¼ (5¼)" long [166.5 (168.5) × 11 (13.5) cm]

MATERIALS

Light Fingering Version:

— Helix by La Bien Aimée [100 g hanks, each approx 710 yds (650 m), 75% Falkland merino wool, 25% Gotland wool]: 1 hank Madeleine (A)
— Size US 8 (5 mm) needles, or size needed to obtain gauge
— Blocking pins

Aran Version:

— Merino Aran by La Bien Aimée [100 g hanks, each approx 182 yds (166 m), 100% superwash merino wool]: 2 hanks Rust (B)
— Size US 10½ (6.5 mm) needles, or size needed to obtain gauge
— Blocking pins

GAUGE

Light Fingering Version: 17 sts and 28 rows = 4" (10 cm) over Tumbling Blocks Lace, using smaller needles and 2 strands of A held together

Aran Version: 15 sts and 22 rows = 4" (10 cm) over Tumbling Blocks Lace, using larger needles and 1 strand of B

NOTES

Instructions are given for Light Fingering Version first, with Aran Version in parentheses; when only one number is given, it applies to both versions.

For Light Fingering Version, use 2 strands of yarn held together for entire piece.

You may work the Tumbling Blocks Lace from either the text or the chart (see pages 16–17).

SCARF

— Using smaller (larger) needles, long-tail CO, and 2 (1) strand(s) of A (B), CO 278 (248) sts.
— Continue with 2 (1) strand(s) of A (B) for remainder of piece.
— Knit 1 row.
— *Next Row (WS):* K2, purl to last 2 sts, k2.
— Work Rows 1–26 of Tumbling Blocks Lace once.
— Knit 1 row.
— *Next Row (WS):* K2, purl to last 2 sts, k2.
— BO all sts purlwise.

FINISHING

Weave in ends. Pin to measurements and steam block. Allow to dry completely before unpinning.

STITCH PATTERN
Tumbling Blocks Lace
(multiple of 10 sts + 18)

- *Row 1 (RS):* K4, yo, ssk, *k8, yo, ssk; rep from * to last 12 sts, k7, k2tog, yo, k3.
- *Row 2:* K2, p2, *yo, p2tog, p5, ssp, yo, p1; rep from * to last 4 sts, p2, k2.
- *Row 3:* K6, *yo, ssk, k3, k2tog, yo, k3; rep from * to last 2 sts, k2.
- *Row 4:* K2, p4, *yo, p2tog, p1, ssp, yo, p5; rep from * to last 2 sts, k2.
- *Row 5:* K3, yo, ssk, k3, *yo, sssk, yo, k7; rep from * to end.
- *Row 6:* K2, p5, ssp, yo, *p3, ssp, yo; rep from * to last 4 sts, p2, k2.
- *Row 7:* K5, *yo, ssk, k3; rep from * to last 3 sts, k3.
- *Row 8:* K2, *p3, ssp, yo; rep from * to last 6 sts, p4, k2.
- *Row 9:* K7, *yo, ssk, k3; rep from * to last st, k1.
- *Row 10:* K2, p1, ssp, yo, *p3, ssp, yo; rep from * to last 3 sts, p1, k2,
- *Row 11:* K4, *yo, ssk, k3; rep from * to last 4 sts, k4.
- *Rows 12–14:* Rep Rows 2–4.
- *Row 15:* K8, *yo, k3tog, yo, k7; rep from * to end.
- *Row 16:* K2, p1, yo, p2tog, *p3, yo, p2tog; rep from * to last 3 sts, p1, k2.
- *Row 17:* K7, *k2tog, yo, k3; rep from * to last st, k1.
- *Row 18:* K2, p3, *yo, p2tog, p3; rep from * to last 3 sts, p1, k2.
- *Row 19:* K5, *k2tog, yo, k3; rep from * to last 3 sts, k3.
- *Row 20:* K2, p5, yo, p2tog, *p3, yo, p2tog; rep from * to last 4 sts, p2, k2.
- *Row 21:* *K3, k2tog, yo; rep from * to last 8 sts, k8.
- *Rows 22–24:* Rep Rows 2–4.
- Row 25: K8, *yo, sssk, yo, k7; rep from * to end.
- *Row 26:* K2, p5, ssp, yo, *p8, ssp, yo; rep from to last 9 sts, p7, k2.

Tumbling Blocks Lace

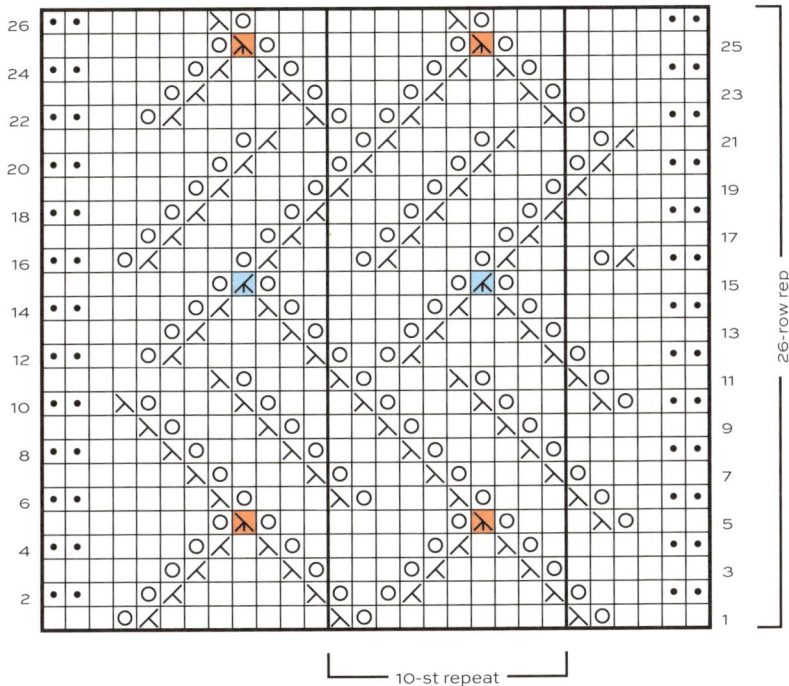

- Knit on RS, purl on WS.
- Knit on WS.
- Yo
- K2tog on RS, p2tog on WS.
- Ssk on RS, ssp on WS.
- K3tog
- Sssk

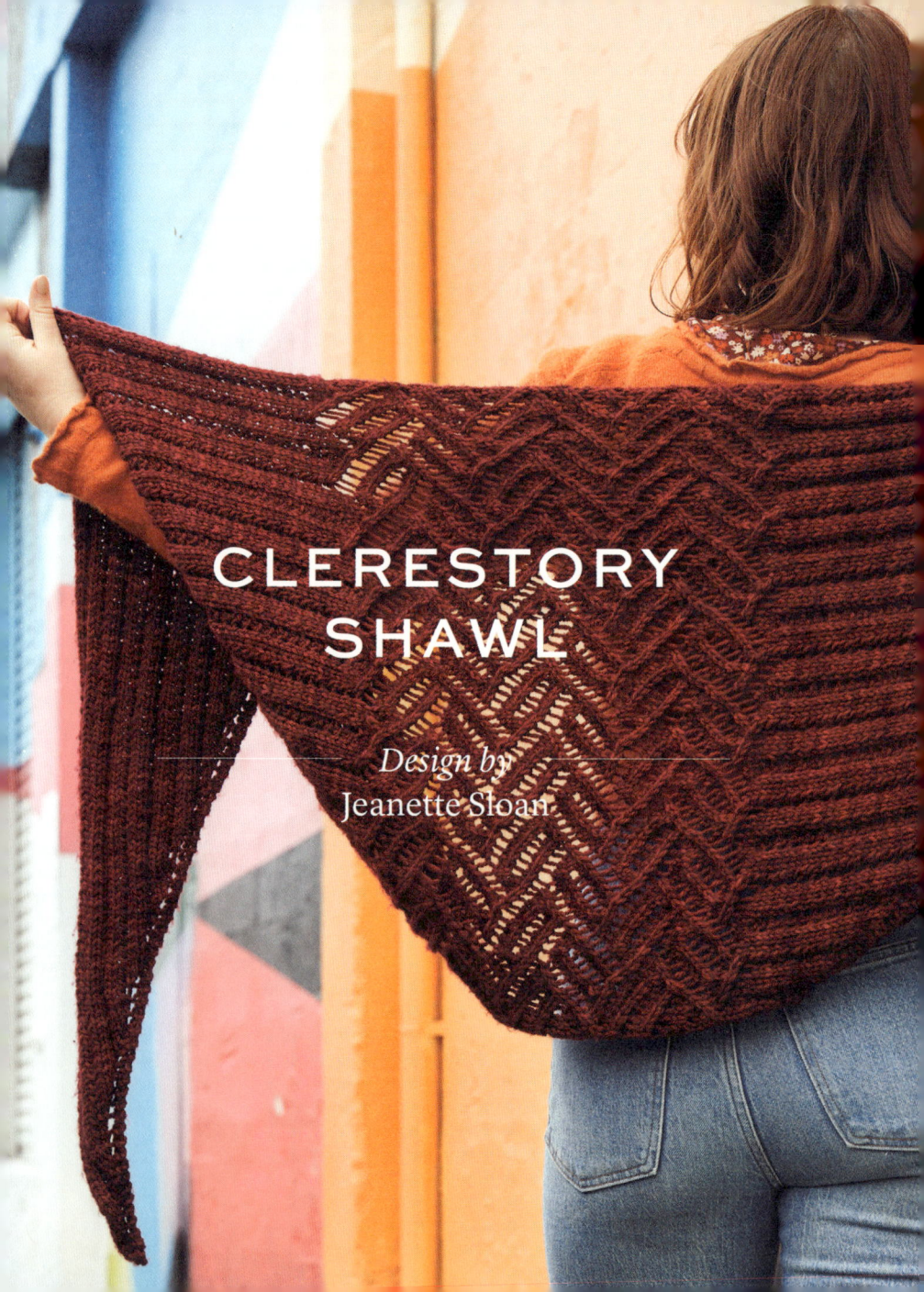

CLERESTORY SHAWL

Design by
Jeanette Sloan

IN TYPICAL JEANETTE SLOAN FASHION, this shawl is full of surprises. She upends the idea of the traditional triangle shawl by eliminating the pointy part, creating a trapezoid shape that is easy to wear and eliminates the possibility of Jemima Puddle-Duck Shawl Syndrome, aka the shawl that points straight to your bum.

Another construction surprise: the shawl is made from point to point, beginning with only four stitches. This allows us to get the hang of the rib lace pattern and the increases in small doses. By the time we arrive at the center panel, we're ready to take on a new lace pattern—a geometric swath of tumbling blocks.

Take your time when you get to the tumbling blocks stitch pattern. The delicate intricacy of the openwork is the result of knitting decreases and yarnovers on both the right and wrong sides. You'll find your sea legs soon enough, no need to rush.

If you want to practice either or both of these lace patterns without having to worry about shaping, start by making the scarves on pages 6 and 12.

KNITTED MEASUREMENTS

72¾ (85¾)" wide × 23¾ (24¼)" long [184.5 (218) cm × 60.5 (61.5) cm]

MATERIALS

Light Fingering Version:
— Helix by La Bien Aimée [100 g hanks, each approx 710 yds (650 m), 75% Falkland merino wool, 25% Gotland wool]: 2 hanks Kokko (A)
— Size US 6 (4 mm) circular needle, 24" (60 cm) long or longer, or size needed to obtain gauge
— Blocking pins

Aran Version:
— Merino Aran by La Bien Aimée [100 g hanks, each approx 182 yds (166 m), 100% superwash merino wool]: 5 hanks Eric Northman (B)
— Size US 10½ (6.5 mm) circular needle, 24" (60 cm) long or longer, or size needed to obtain gauge
— Blocking pins

GAUGE

Light Fingering Version: 23 sts and 35 rows = 4" (10 cm) over Tumbling Blocks Lace, using A and smaller needle, after blocking

Aran Version: 16 sts and 20½ rows = 4" (10 cm) over Tumbling Blocks Lace, using B and larger needle, after blocking

NOTES

Instructions are given for Light Fingering Version first, with Aran Version in parentheses; when only one number is given, it applies to both versions.

Piece is worked back and forth on circular needle to accommodate large number of stitches.

See charts for both lace patterns on pages 22–24.

SHAWL

— Using smaller (larger) needle, long-tail CO, and A (B), CO 4 sts.
— Beg Rib Lace A; work Rows 1–26 once, Rows 27–46 twelve (8) times, then Rows 47–50 once—137 (97) sts after Row 47.
— Beg Tumbling Blocks Lace; work Rows 1 and 2 once, Rows 3–22 four (3) times, then Rows 23–26 once.
— Beg Rib Lace B; work Rows 1–4 once, Rows 5–24 twelve (8) times, then Rows 25–50 once—4 sts remain after Row 49.
— BO all sts.

FINISHING

Weave in ends. Pin to measurements; steam block. Dry completely before unpinning.

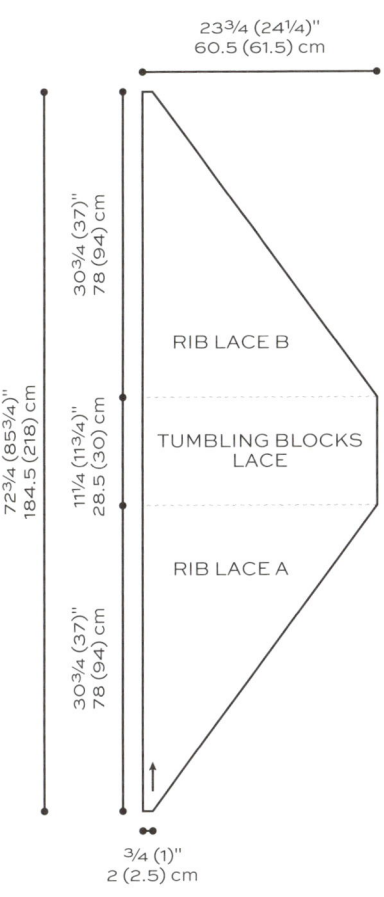

This shawl is worked from one narrow end, with all increases worked along the right edge of Rib Lace A, through the wide center panel (Tumbling Blocks Lace), then to the opposite narrow end, with all decreases worked along the right edge of Rib Lace B.

Rib Lace A

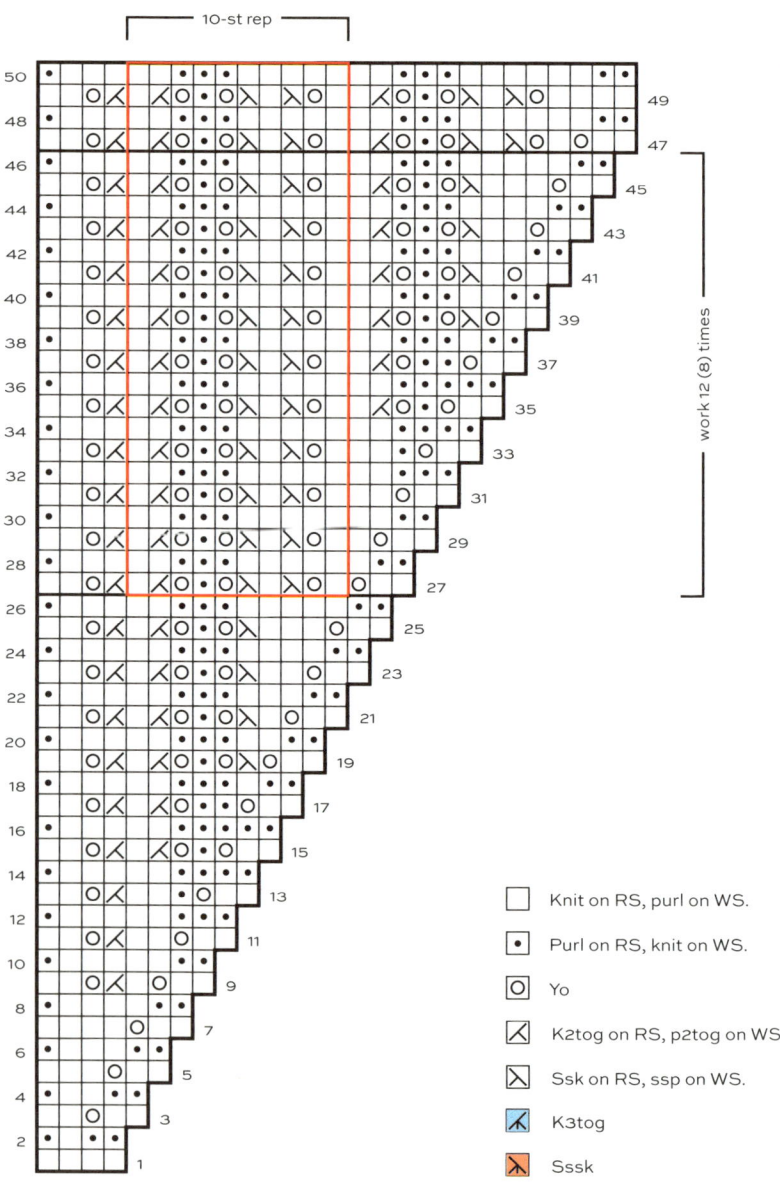

Tumbling Blocks Lace

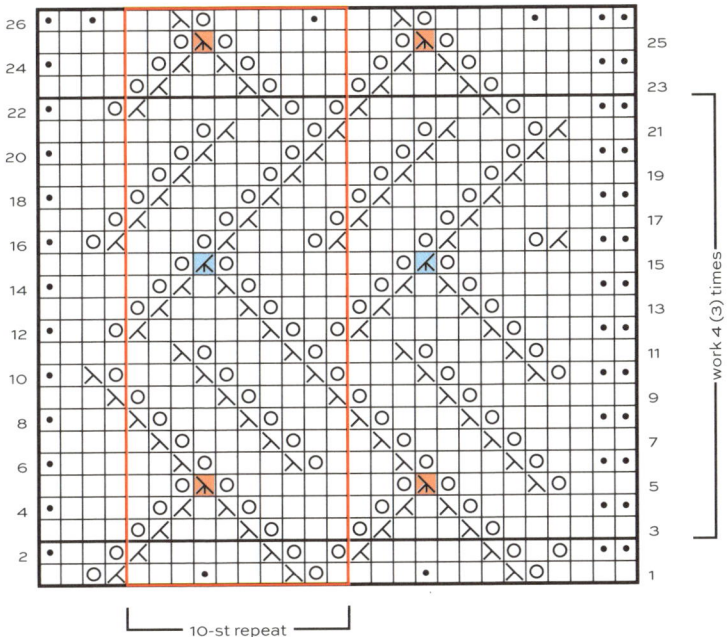

10-st repeat

work 4 (3) times

Rib Lace B

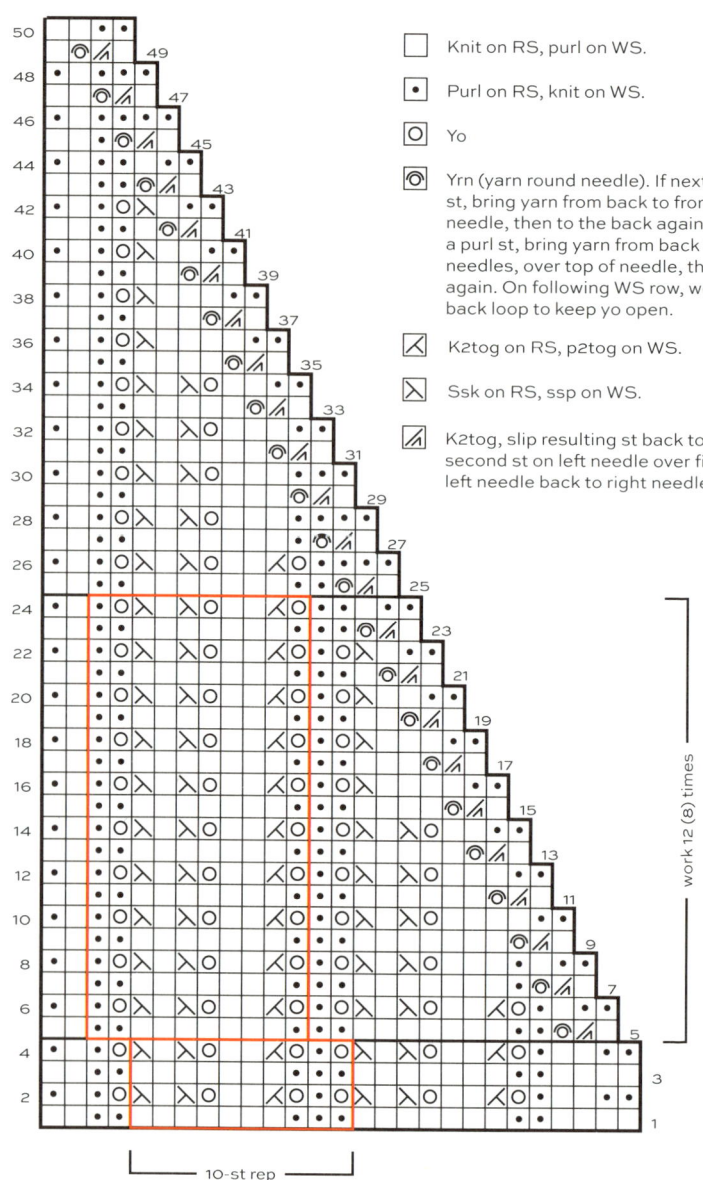

APERTURE STOLE

Design by
Jeanette Sloan

This stole is a billowy, light, and enveloping confection that melds two different yarns (in three different colors). Jeanette chose a lace pattern that looks random (even though it isn't), then added in the extra effect of changing the way the yarns are combined, resulting in exciting oscillations of color, texture, and motif.

The chart requires a bit of focus, but you can do it. Feel free to alter the striping; making it random (rather than following exactly what is shown here) means that you'll have one less detail to follow on the chart, plus your result will be truly one-of-a-kind.

KNITTED MEASUREMENTS

17¼" wide × 72" long (44 × 183 cm)

MATERIALS

- Helix by La Bien Aimée [100 g hanks, each approx 710 yds (650 m), 75% Falkland merino wool, 25% Gotland wool]: 1 hank The Hotness (A)
- Kumo by La Bien Aimée [50 g hanks, each approx 328 yds (300 m), 74% suri alpaca, 26% mulberry silk]: 2 hanks The Hotness (C); 1 hank Tang (B)
- Size US 6 (4 mm) needles, or size needed to obtain gauge
- Stitch markers
- Row counter (optional)
- Blocking pins

GAUGE

21 sts and 31 rows = 4" (10 cm) over Oscillating Lace, using 1 strand of A

NOTES

You may work the Oscillating Lace from either the text or the chart (see pages 30–33). You may wish to use a row counter to keep track of the Stripe Pattern (see page 31).

STOLE

- Using long-tail CO and 1 strand each of A and B held tog, CO 90 sts.
- *Next Row (RS):* Sl 2 purlwise wyib, [k37, pm] twice, knit to end.
- *Next Row:* Sl 2 purlwise wyif, purl to end.
- Cut B; continue with 1 strand of A only.
- Beg Stripe Pattern.
- *Row 1 (RS):* Sl 2 purlwise wyib, work Oscillating Lace to last 2 sts, k2.
- *Row 2:* Sl 2 purlwise wyif, work Oscillating Lace to last 2 sts, p2.
- Work even until you have worked Rows 1–98 of both Stripe Pattern and Oscillating Lace 5 times, then work Rows 1–64 of Stripe Pattern and Oscillating Lace once more.
- Cut A and join second strand of C; continue with 2 strands of C held tog.
- *Next Row (RS):* Sl 2 purlwise wyib, knit to end.
- *Next Row:* Sl 2 purlwise wyif, purl to end.
- BO all sts purlwise.

FINISHING

Weave in ends. Pin to measurements and steam block. Allow to dry completely before unpinning.

STITCH PATTERN
Oscillating Lace

Note: The row numbers on which Stripe Pattern color changes occur are circled in red. (panel of 86 sts)

- *Rows 1, 17, 33, and 49 (RS):* [K14, k2tog, yo, (k6, k2tog, yo) twice, k5, sm] twice, k1, k2tog, yo, k6, k2tog, yo, k1.
- *Row 2 and all WS Rows through Row 64:* Purl.
- *Rows 3, 19, 35, and 51:* [K13, (k2tog, yo, k6) 3 times, sm] twice, k2tog, yo, k6, k2tog, yo, k2.
- *Rows 5, 21, 37, and 53:* [K4, k2tog, yo, k6, k2tog, yo, k14, k2tog, yo, k7, sm] twice, k7, k2tog, yo, k3.
- *Rows 7, 23, 39, and 55:* [K3, k2tog, yo, (k6, k2tog, yo) 3 times, k8, sm] twice, k6, k2tog, yo, k4.
- *Rows 9, 25, 41, and 57:* [K2, k2tog, yo, (k6, k2tog, yo) 3 times, k9, sm] twice, k5, k2tog, yo, k5.
- *Rows 11, 27, 43, and 59:* [K1, k2tog, yo, (k6, k2tog, yo) 3 times, k10, sm] twice, k4, k2tog, yo, k6.
- *Rows 13, 29, 45, and 61:* [K2tog, yo, (k6, k2tog, yo) 3 times, k11, sm] twice, k3, k2tog, yo, k7.
- *Rows 15, 31, 47, and 63:* [K7, k2tog, yo, (k6, k2tog, yo) 3 times, k4, sm] twice, k2, k2tog, yo, k6, k2tog, yo.
- *Row 65:* [(K6, k2tog, yo) 4 times, k5, sm] twice, k1, k2tog, yo, k6, k2tog, yo, k1.
- *Row 66:* P2, yo, p2tog, p1, ssp, yo, p3, yo, p2tog, [sm, (p1, ssp, yo, p3, yo, p2tog) 3 times, p13] twice.
- *Rows 67 and 79:* K12, k2tog, yo, [k5, yo, s2kp2, yo] twice, k5, yo, ssk, sm, k12, k2tog, yo, [k5, yo, s2kp2, yo] 4 times (replacing marker after s2kp2 when encountered), k3.
- *Rows 68 and 80:* P2, ssp, yo, p1, yo, p2tog, p3, ssp, yo, [sm, (p1, yo, p2tog, p3, ssp, yo) 3 times, p13] twice.
- *Rows 69 and 81:* [K13, (yo, ssk, k3, k2tog, yo, k1) 3 times, sm] twice, yo, ssk, k3, k2tog, yo, k1, yo, ssk, k2.
- *Rows 70 and 82:* Rep Row 68.
- *Rows 71 and 83:* Rep Row 69.
- *Rows 72 and 84:* P1, ssp, yo, p3, yo, p2tog, p1, ssp, yo, p1, [sm, p2, yo, p2tog, p1, ssp, yo (p3, yo, p2tog, p1, ssp, yo) twice, p14] twice.
- *Rows 73 and 85:* [K15, yo, s2kp2, yo, (k5, yo, s2kp2, yo) twice, k3, sm] twice, k2, yo, s2kp2, yo, k5, yo, ssk.
- *Rows 74 and 86:* P1, yo, p2tog, p3, ssp, yo, p1, yo, p2tog, p1, [sm, p2, ssp, yo, p1, yo, p2tog, (p3, ssp, yo, p1, yo, p2tog) twice, p14] twice.

- *Rows 75 and 87:* [K14, k2tog, yo, k1, yo, ssk, (k3, k2tog, yo, k1, yo, ssk) twice, k2, sm] twice, k1, k2tog, yo, k1, yo, ssk, k3, k2tog, yo, k1.
- *Rows 76 and 88:* Rep Row 74.
- *Rows 77 and 89:* Rep Row 75.
- *Rows 78 and 90:* P2, yo, p2tog, p1, ssp, yo, p3, yo, p2tog, [sm, (p1, ssp, yo, p3, yo, p2tog) 3 times, p13] twice.
- *Row 91:* Rep Row 67.
- *Row 92:* P2, ssp, yo, p1, yo, p2tog, p3, ssp, yo, [sm, p1, yo, p2tog, (p3, ssp, yo, p1, yo, p2tog) twice, p18] twice.
- *Row 93:* [K18, k2tog, yo, k1, yo, ssk, k3, k2tog, yo, k1, yo, ssk, k6, sm] twice, yo, ssk, k3, k2tog, yo, k1, yo, ssk, k2.
- *Row 94:* P2, ssp, yo, p1, yo, p2tog, p3, ssp, yo, [sm, p6, ssp, yo, p1, yo, p2tog, p3, ssp, yo, p1, yo, p2tog, p18] twice.
- *Row 95:* [K13, yo, ssk, (k3, k2tog, yo, k1, yo, ssk) twice, k6, sm] twice, yo, ssk, k3, k2tog, yo, k1, yo, ssk, k2.
- *Row 96:* Rep Row 72.
- *Row 97:* [K15, yo, s2kp2, yo, (k5, yo, s2kp2, yo) twice, k3, sm] twice, k2, yok s2kp2, yo, k5, yo, ssk.
- *Row 98:* Yo, p2tog, p6, yo, p2tog, p2, [sm, p4, yo, p2tog, (p6, yo, p2tog) twice, p15] twice.
- Rep Rows 1-98 for Oscillating Lace.

Stripe Pattern

Note: Stripe Pattern color change rows are circled on the Oscillating Lace written instructions and on the chart.

- *Rows 1-22:* Work with 1 strand of A.
- *Rows 23-28:* Work with 1 strand of C.
- *Rows 29-44:* Work with 1 strand of A.
- *Rows 45 and 46:* Work with 1 strand each of A and B held tog.
- *Rows 47-52:* Work with 1 strand of A.
- *Rows 53-66:* Work with 1 strand each of A and C held tog.
- *Rows 67-98:* Work with 1 strand of C for all vertical repeats except the final repeat; for final repeat, work with 1 strand of B.
- Rep Rows 1-98 for Stripe Pattern.

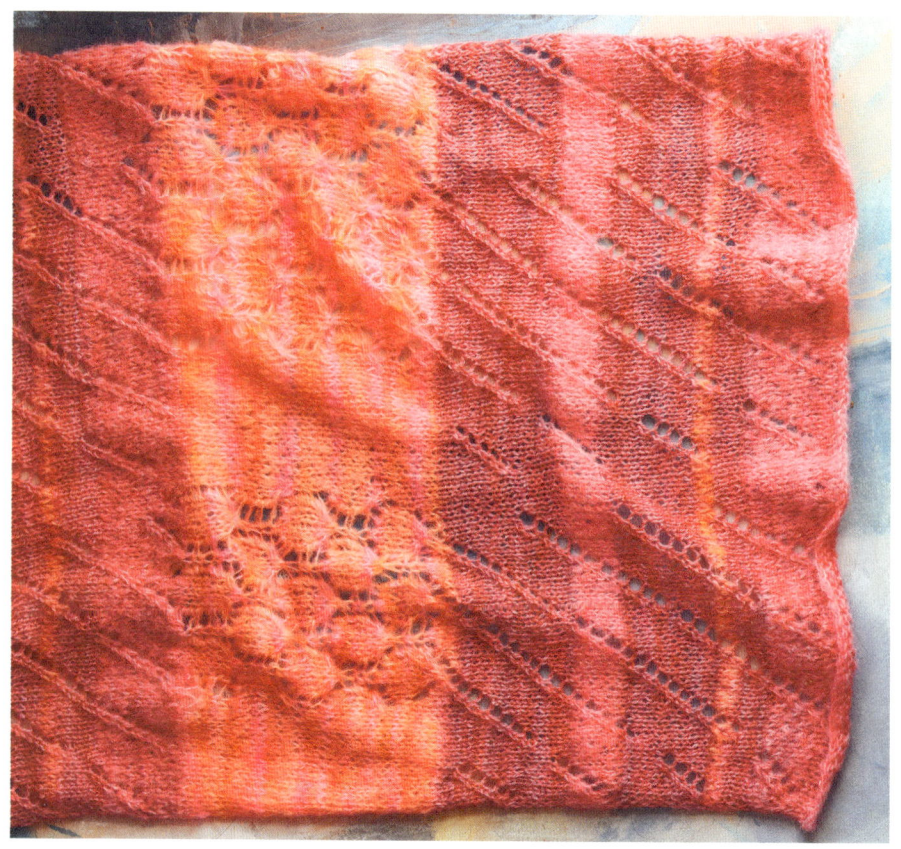

Chart Note

All row numbers are given to make it easier to match Oscillating Lace rows to Stripe Pattern rows; Stripe Pattern color change rows are circled in red.

☐	Knit on RS, purl on WS.
O	Yo
╱	K2tog on RS, p2tog on WS.
╲	Ssk on RS, ssp on WS.
⋏	S2kp2
⋏	Work as ssk the first time this is worked; work as s2kp2 the second time this is worked.

Oscillating Lace

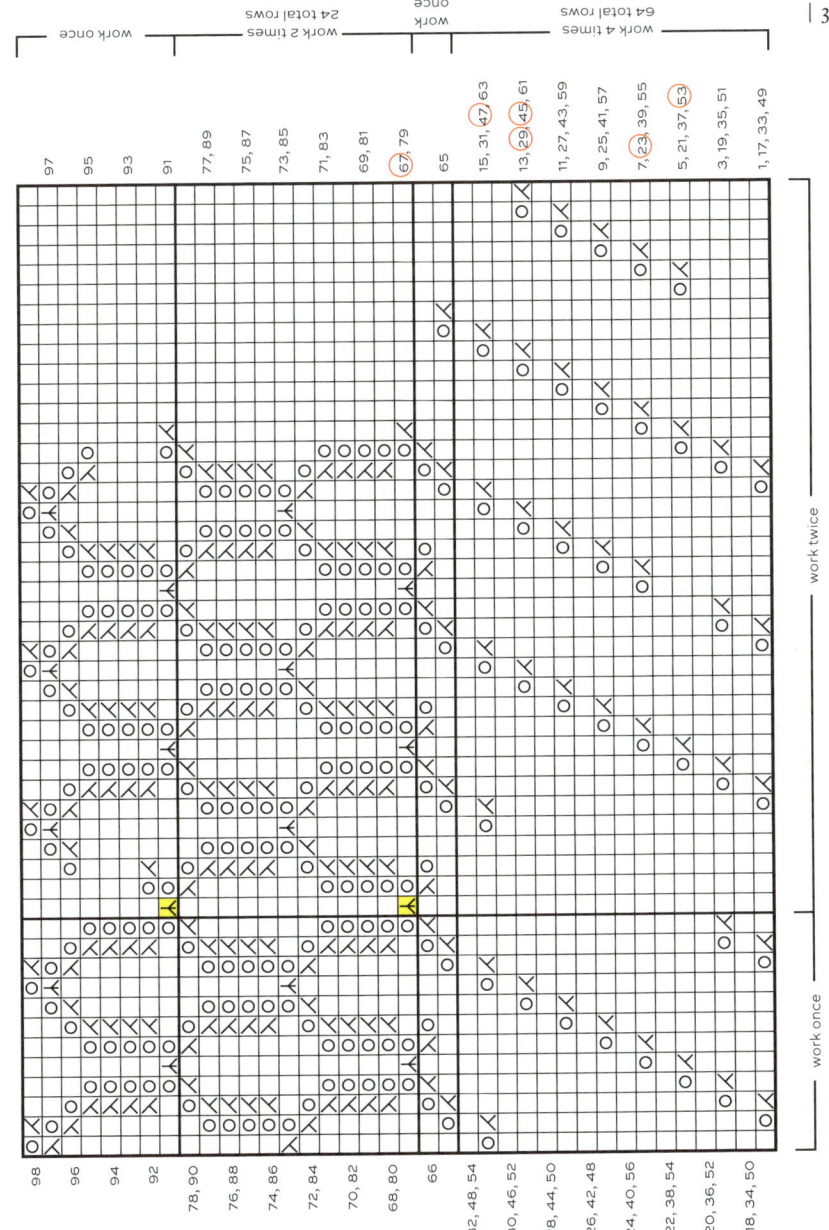

WE KNOW KNITTED LACE when we see it: an often elaborate arrangement of threads with holes strategically placed in decorative patterns. Knitters celebrate the knitted lace of many different places: the Shetland Islands, the Orenburg region of Russia, Estonia.

The popularity of lace has ebbed and flowed over the years, but there have always been knitters fascinated by it. Some work devotedly on special pieces for rituals like baptisms and weddings or for their homes; others still find places for it in their wardrobes. We've done double takes at the frilly-shawl-over-sweatpants looks worn jubilantly at fiber festivals, but we love it, truly.

In a time of stripped-down modernism, lace could be seen as old-fashioned, but the ways to wear it have evolved. While it used to seem destined for formal occasions—worn to put the spotlight on its intricacies and the time it took to achieve them—these days it also feels good to wear our lace knitting in a nonchalant, almost subversive way: We might wrap a lace shawl over a special dress—or fling it over athleisurewear, or scrunch it inside the collar of a denim jacket.

In letting lace take its place in our daily wardrobes, we keep what we love alive.

MOOD CARDIGAN

Design by
Jeanette Sloan

THE IDEA FOR THIS SOFTLY STRUCTURED CARDIGAN came from a machine-knit linen sweater Jeanette bought nearly a decade ago and has been wearing ever since.

When worn with the rib framing the neck, the lacy body hangs over the hips (see left); when turned upside down, that same fabric softly cascades to just past the waist (see pages 5 and 45).

Jeanette's eye for just-right details—a textural lace pattern, mitered ribbing, a tubular bind-off at the cuff—elevates the Mood Cardigan beyond the realm of any store-bought garment and makes it especially satisfying to knit. It's wearable—and practical—art, extraordinary and everyday at the same time.

KNITTED MEASUREMENTS

Back width: 36½ (39, 41½, 44)" [92.5 (99, 105.5, 112) cm]
Length: 24¾ (25½, 26¼, 27)" [63 (65, 66.5, 68.5) cm]

SIZES

To fit bust sizes 30–36 (38–44, 46–52, 54–60)" [76–91.5 (96.5–112, 117–132, 137–152.5) cm]

MATERIALS

- Helix by La Bien Aimée [100 g hanks, each approx 710 yds (650 m), 75% Falkland merino wool, 25% Gotland wool]: 4 (4,4,5) hanks Yellow Brick Road (A)
- Size 8 (5 mm) circular needle, 32" (80 cm) long or longer, or size needed to obtain gauge
- Size 9 (5.5 mm) or larger needle in any style, for body panel BO
- Size 7 (4.5 mm) circular needles, 16" (40 cm) and 32" (80 cm) long
- Crochet hook size US H-8 (5 mm)
- Removable markers
- Waste yarn
- Blocking pins

GAUGE

17½ sts and 27½ rows = 4" (10 cm) over Alternating Lace using size US 8 (5 mm) needle and 2 strands of A held tog

NOTES

The cardigan is worked with 2 strands of yarn held together throughout.
The piece is worked back and forth on a circular needle to accommodate the large number of stitches.
You may work the Alternating Lace from either the text or the chart (see right).

STITCH PATTERNS

Alternating Lace (multiple of 6 sts + 7)
— *Row 1 (RS):* K2, yo, sk2p, yo, *k3, yo, sk2p, yo; rep from * to 2 last sts, k2.
— *Row 2:* K1, purl to last st, k1.
— *Rows 3-8:* Rep Rows 1 and 2 three times.
— *Row 9:* K5, *yo, sk2p, yo, k3; rep from * to last 2 sts, k2.
— *Row 10:* K1, purl to last st, k1.
— *Rows 11-16:* Rep Rows 9 and 10 three times.
— Rep Rows 1-16 for Alternating Lace.

Circular 1x1 Rib (even number of sts)
— *All Rnds:* *K1, p1; rep from * to end.

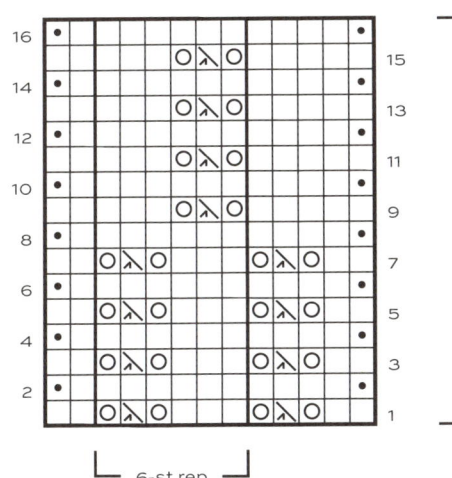

Alternating Lace

☐ Knit on RS, purl on WS.

• Knit on WS.

○ Yo

⟋ Sk2p

This cardigan is constructed of two rectangular panels. The sleeve panel begins with a provisional cast on and is worked from end to end. After blocking, stitches are picked up for the sleeve cuffs and worked in the round. The body panel is worked from the bottom up, then bound off. After blocking, the piece is folded to create a back and two fronts. The bound-off edge of the back portion of the body is then sewn to one long edge of the sleeve panel, and the remaining bound-off edges of each front portion are sewn to the opposite edges of the sleeve panel. The front band/collar is picked up along the center front opening and worked flat in ribbing. If you are having trouble visualizing the construction, see photo on page 43.

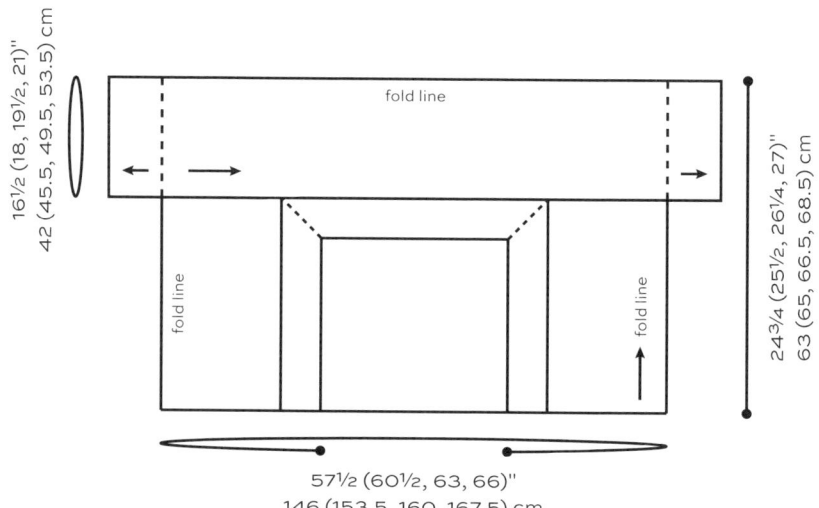

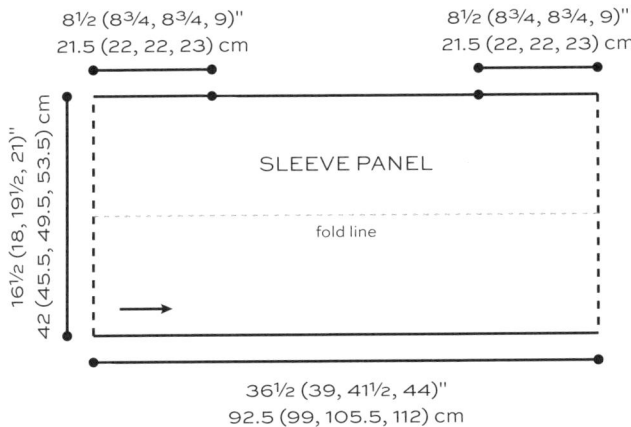
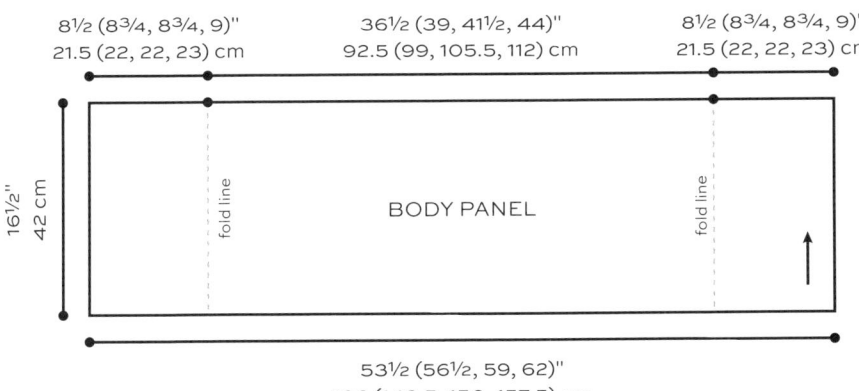

SLEEVE PANEL

- Using crochet hook, waste yarn, and provisional CO method (see page 44), CO 73 (79, 85, 91) sts.
- Change to 2 strands of yarn held tog and size US 8 (5 mm) needle.
- Work in Alternating Lace until piece measures approx 36½ (39, 41½, 44)" [92.5 (99, 105.5, 112) cm], ending with Row 8 or 16 of pattern. Cut yarn, place sts on waste yarn, and set aside.

BODY PANEL

- Using 2 strands of yarn held tog and size US 8 (5 mm) needle, CO 235 (247, 259, 271) sts.
- Work in Alternating Lace until piece measures approx 16½" (42 cm), ending with Row 8 or 16 of pattern.
- Cut yarn, leaving a tail 4 times the width of the piece, place sts on waste yarn, and set aside.

FINISHING

Weave in ends. Pin pieces to measurements and steam block. Allow to dry completely before unpinning.

BODY PANEL

- Return sts to size US 8 (5 mm) circular needle. With RS facing, using size US 9 (5.5 mm) or larger needle and yarn attached to panel, BO all sts loosely knitwise, making sure that BO edge does not pull in.

SLEEVE CUFFS

Return live sleeve sts to smaller 16" (40 cm) circular needle. Join; pm for beg of rnd and work in the rnd as follows:

- With 2 strands of yarn held tog, work Circular 1×1 Rib, until ribbing measures 2" (5 cm), dec 1 st on first rnd.
- BO all sts using Tubular BO (see page 44) or your preferred stretchy BO.
- Carefully unzip provisional CO from opposite end of sleeve and place sts on smaller 16" (40 cm) circular needle. Work as for opposite cuff.
- Place marker 8½ (8¾, 8¾, 9)" [21.5 (22, 22, 23) cm] in from each side edge of body panel, along BO edge, and the same distance in from top of each cuff along one edge of sleeve panel (see schematic). With RS of pieces facing, beg and ending at top of ribbed cuffs, sew unmarked edge of sleeve panel between markers on body panel (see assembly diagram).

Sew remaining edges of body panel to other side edge of sleeve panel, from cuff to marker on each side.

FRONT BANDS AND COLLAR

With 2 strands of yarn held tog and smaller 32" (80 cm) circular needle, beg at lower right front edge, pick up and knit approx 3 sts for every 4 rows along right front edge, making sure you pick up an even number of sts; pick up and knit 1 st in corner at seam, place removable marker around st; pick up and knit approx 3 sts for every 4 rows along neck edge, making sure you pick up an odd number of sts; pick up and knit 1 st in corner at seam, place removable marker around st; pick up and knit approx 3 sts for every 4 rows along left front edge, making sure you pick up an even number of sts.

- *Set-Up Row 1 (WS):* *P1, k1; rep from * to last st, p1.
- *Dec Row (RS):* Knitting the knit sts and purling the purl sts as they face you, [work to 1 st before marked st, s2kp2] twice, work to end—4 sts dec.
- *Next Row:* Knit the knit sts and purl the purl sts as they face you.
- Rep last 2 rows until ribbing measures 2" (5 cm).
- BO all sts loosely in pattern.

SPECIAL TECHNIQUES FOR MOOD CARDIGAN

Provisional CO (Crochet onto Needle):

— Make slip knot with waste yarn; place on crochet hook.
— Hold spare needle in left hand, pointing up, and crochet hook in right hand; hold both yarn ends behind needle with left hand, with working end of yarn over left index finger. *Take crochet hook across front of needle, go under working end of waste yarn from left to right, catch yarn, and draw through loop on crochet hook to create 1 st on needle; take working end of yarn over needle tip to back again.
— Repeat from * until you have cast on required number of sts. Work a few crochet chain sts to indicate which end of cast-on to undo to unravel it, then cut yarn and draw tail through loop on crochet hook to fasten off.
— When ready to work live sts, unravel cast on, beginning with crochet chain end, and unzip chain, placing live sts on a spare needle as you unzip.

Tubular BO:

— *Tubular Rnd 1*: *K1, sl 1 purlwise wyif; rep from * to end.
— *Tubular Rnd 2*: *Sl 1 purlwise wyib, p1; rep from * to end. Cut yarn, leaving a tail 4 times the circumference of the ribbing.
— On the following rnd, you will divide knit and purl sts onto separate needles. Use working needle as front needle and size US 7 (4.5 mm) 32" (80 cm) long circular needle as back needle. Do not knit or purl sts on this rnd.
— *Tubular Rnd 3 (non-knitting rnd)*: *Sl 1 knit st to front needle, sl 1 purl st to back needle; rep from * to end. All knit sts should now be on front needle and all purl sts should be on back needle. Graft front and back sts tog using Kitchener st.

Kitchener Stitch:
- Using a blunt tapestry needle, thread a length of yarn approximately 4 times the length of the section to be joined.
- With stitches still on the needles, hold the pieces to be joined parallel, with WSs together, both needle tips pointing to the right. Working from right to left:

Setup
- Insert tapestry needle into first stitch on front needle purlwise, pull yarn through, leaving stitch on needle.
- Insert tapestry needle into first stitch on back needle knitwise, pull yarn through, leaving stitch on needle.

Repeat for all stitches
- *Insert tapestry needle into first stitch on front needle knitwise, pull yarn through, remove stitch from needle.
- Insert tapestry needle into next stitch on front needle purlwise, pull yarn through, leave stitch on needle.
- Insert tapestry needle into first stitch on back needle purlwise, pull yarn through, remove stitch from needle.
- Insert tapestry needle into next stitch on back needle knitwise, pull yarn through, leave stitch on needle.
- Repeat from *, adjusting stitch tension every 3 or 4 stitches to match the pieces being joined.
- When 1 stitch remains on each needle, cut yarn and pass through last 2 stitches to fasten off.

MEET JEANETTE SLOAN

Jeanette Sloan is a British knitwear designer who lives in the city of Brighton and Hove, on the south coast of England. Her multifaceted career has included designing hand- and machine-knit and embroidered fabrics for ready-to-wear; creating patterns and yarns for hand-knitters; owning and managing a yarn shop; and writing for the UK's *Knitting Magazine*. In spring 2020, she launched BIPOCinfiber.com, an online resource portal that amplifies and celebrates the work of black, indigenous and people of color in the fiber industry.

You come from a very creative family.
My father was a shoemaker before he moved from Barbados to London and became an electrician. He often designed and made furniture for his own enjoyment when he wasn't working. My mother was an amazing knitter and sewer, and she could also crochet and tat well. My brother has fantastic drawing skills, and it was his encouragement that inspired me to start drawing. From a young age, I knew I had to do something creative, too. My father told me that I was always inquisitive about how stuff was put together.

What are some of your most vivid memories of being creative during your childhood?
I remember my mother teaching me to knit when I was seven. My first project was a red acrylic doll scarf. I also remember constructing a cardboard dollhouse. I made everything: chairs and table, even a saucepan with a cocktail-stick handle that sat on the cardboard stove—with rice in it!

I was a member of the batik club in junior high, and in high school I did ceramics and printmaking.

What does this Field Guide's "Open" theme mean for you?
Of course, there is the knitterly interpretation of open stitches, or lace. For the projects I designed for this Field Guide, I wanted to break open people's conception of what lace could be.

I like the idea of being open-minded: open to new ways of looking at how we knit and what we knit, the colors and patterns we combine, the yarns we choose, the direction we knit in—and, much more broadly, how we move through and interpret the world around us.

You had two (fortunately, non-cancerous) brain tumors removed a few years ago. How did that experience affect your way of moving through the world?
I have to do everything more slowly now, so I'm trying to embrace the benefits of that rather than fighting it. Slowing down as a designer means I can pay more attention to small details that elevate what I create. For example, I enjoyed taking extra time to figure out how to do the ribbed miter on the border of the Mood Cardigan (see page 36).

I also liked playing with different ways of achieving a sense of randomness and asymmetry within a repeating pattern for the Aperture Stole (see page 26).

I don't know if this is a result of my brain surgery (or just getting older and more confident), but I'm embracing my love of hot, vibrant colors and clashing patterns. In the past I didn't like calling attention to myself, but now I'm ok with it. I'm certainly learning the importance of self-care, which for me means taking a step back from the noise of social media and spending more time reading, cooking, gardening, and making things purely for the pleasure of the creative process.

I want to be doing more personal knitting. I would love to be knitting from someone else's patterns. It's not only more relaxing, but there is no pressure to remember everything and write it all down.

ABBREVIATIONS

Beg: Begin(ning)(s)
BO: Bind off
CO: Cast on
K: Knit
K2tog: Knit 2 stitches together. 1 stitch decreased.
K3tog: Knit 3 stitches together. 2 stitches decreased.
P: Purl
P2tog: Purl 2 stitches together. 1 stitch decreased.
Pm: Place marker
Rep: Repeat(ed)(ing)(s)
RS: Right side
S2kp2: Slip next 2 stitches to right needle together as if to knit 2 together, knit 1 stitch, pass 2 slipped stitches over. 2 stitches decreased.
Sk2p: Slip 1 knitwise, knit 2 together, pass slipped stitch over. 2 stitches decreased.
Sl: Slip
Sm: Slip marker
Ssk: Slip 1 stitch knitwise, slip 1 stitch purlwise, insert left needle into front of these 2 stitches and knit together from this position. 1 stitch decreased.
Sssk: Slip 1 stitch knitwise, slip 2 stitches one at a time purlwise, insert left needle into the front of these 3 stitches and knit them together from this position. 2 stitches decreased.
Ssp: Slip 1 stitch knitwise, slip 1 stitch purlwise, insert left needle into the front of these 2 stitches and knit them together from this position. 1 stitch decreased.
St(s): Stitch(es)
Tog: Together
WS: Wrong side
Wyib: With yarn in back
Wyif: With yarn in front
Yo: Yarnover